BAREFOOT

Barefoot

KEVIN HART

University of Notre Dame Press

Notre Dame, Indiana

Published by the University of Notre Dame Press
Notre Dame, Indiana 46556
undpress.nd.edu

Cover image: *Feet on Rug*, by Philip Guston, 1978.
Oil on canvas, 203.2 x 264.2 cm / 80 x 104 inches
© The Estate of Philip Guston, courtesy Hauser & Wirth.

Library of Congress Cataloging-in-Publication Data

Names: Hart, Kevin, 1954– author.
Title: Barefoot / Kevin Hart.
Description: Notre Dame, Indiana : University of Notre Dame Press, [2018] |
    Identifiers: LCCN 2017055865 (print) | LCCN 2017060914 (ebook) | ISBN
    9780268103156 (pdf) | ISBN 9780268103163 (epub) | ISBN 9780268103132
    (hardcover : alk. paper) | ISBN 0268103135 (hardcover : alk. paper) | ISBN
    9780268103149 (pbk. : alk. paper) | ISBN 0268103143 (pbk. : alk. paper)
Classification: LCC PR9619.3.H3336 (ebook) | LCC PR9619.3.H3336 A6 2018
    (print) | DDC 821/.914—dc23
LC record available at https://lccn.loc.gov/2017055865

∞ *This paper meets the requirements of ANSI/NISO Z39.48-1992*
(Permanence of Paper).

for
TONY KELLY

Después,
Hay que seguir descalzo.
—Roberto Juarroz

CONTENTS

4

5

ACKNOWLEDGMENTS

Poems in this collection have appeared in *The Anglican Theological Review,* *Antipodes, Arena, The Australian, Australian Financial Review, The Canberra Times, The Chronicle of Higher Education, Commonweal, Eco-Theo Review, First Things, Hudson Review, Humanities Australia, Notre Dame Review, Southerly, The Sun Herald, Two Thirds North, Virginia Quarterly Review,* and *Westerly.* "Little Book of Mourning" was reprinted in *Best Australian Poems 2013* (Black Inc.), "Apart" was reprinted in *Best Australian Poems 2014* (Black Inc.), and "Summer in Melbourne" was reprinted in *Best Australian Poems 2015* (Black Inc.). Several poems appeared in *The Second Genesis,* ed. Anuraag Sharma (ARAWL1, 2014), *The Turnow Anthology of Contemporary Australian Poetry,* ed. John Kinsella (Turnow Books, 2014), and in my *Wild Track: New and Selected Poems* (University of Notre Dame Press, 2015). Some poems appeared in Spanish, translated by Roberto Vivero, in *Descalzo* (Madrid: Ápeiron Editions, Colección Clavileño, 2016). I would like to thank Robert Gray, Paul Kane, Jean-Yves Lacoste, Susan Stewart, Henry Weinfield, and Charles Wright for their comments on poems in an earlier version of the book.

1

NIGHTS

Dark One, I walk the streets for half the night
And see my father slide toward the grave:
Look left, and death will enter from the right

Or jump on you from some tremendous height
No matter if you run or act all brave.
Dark One, I walk the streets for half the night,

Not looking flash, not looking for a fight.
A car screams through a light: a nasty shave.
Look left, and death will enter from the right,

And if he passes it's no oversight.
He whispers, "Go, get all that you must crave."
Dark One, I walk the streets for half the night,

Not looking for the very things I might,
Not looking for the years that you once gave.
Look left, and death will enter from the right.

My father's crawling upward to your light,
I tell myself, while counting years to save.
Dark One, I walk the streets for half the night.
Look left, and death will enter from the right.

LITTLE BOOK OF MOURNING

in memoriam JHH

Winter

Dark freeze in Charlottesville;
The drinking water bites my lip.

Bare room: I write till dusk
In dusty radiator heat.

Clocks graze on me all day;
I hear the silence of two crows

Then look down at my arm:
Not even your shadow's there to touch.

Inside

I only speak old words:
They keep in with the dead,
They leave their doors ajar.

Some words are corridors
That lead us to the dead
And we can trust their dark;

We pass a hammer, sure,
We pass an anvil too,
We pass a stirrup last;

And then we find the dead
Curled up, inside, asleep,
Our names upon their tongues.

On the Mantelpiece

My father doesn't know
That he died years ago:
He looks out for a while

From '65 or so
And I look back, although
It chills away my smile

To see him with a glow
At dinner, in the snow,
In full-on sixties style

Not knowing then the blow
That was to knock him low,
That scrapes me like a file.

Parachuting

They dropped you into France when young,
A town up north (I went there once);

Your squad was braced behind a wall
And you could see the man in front

Go left and his big head go right,
And saw yourself from up above,

And lived the moment in a vise
And stayed there almost fifty years.

You showed me medals only once
And a weird wound just once as well,

A mucky hole that sucked in flesh
On each side of an upper thigh.

Now you've gone down again at night:
No river and no fields beneath.

Downstairs

I walk down there
Because I must
And feel each step
Is less than just

And blank a thought
But can't ignore
A shadow's sigh
The furnace roar

This is the place
Where darkness grows
This is the place
My father goes

BAREFOOT

Still of our world, dear father, in your grave
Or at my winter window, looking hard
Into a life you never knew in life:

This house of books, this fire that cracks a whip
At cats and shadows when they cross the room,
Vast silences that swallow days alive.

Dear father, know another life, your own,
Not of this world, seen faintly through past love
As though it were a frosted windowpane,

Know you can go there, to that other world,
By walking barefoot in the dark tonight,
As happened all the time at home in time

With just a fraying God to keep you warm
On winter nights, in Brisbane, in the nights
You couldn't sleep for memories of war,

Know in that other world you are your life,
Complete, intact, and brimming high with love;
Know nothing comes undone there, not a thing.

Faint shadows gather in the afternoon
Around a house, around a fighting fire;
Look past them all, look through the icy rain,

A night not of this world yet drawing close,
Come from a time that's hollowed of all time.
Don't sleep tonight, dear father, darkness eats

Shadows and men alive, just walk barefoot
Into that other world: no darkness there,
All warm, in silences and words, all warm.

FATHER

My father's only still a child in death.
So can he speak that quiet language now?
And can he walk the ways they slowly teach?

And does he smell thin summer here below?
So questions flicker through a hot dry day
When summer leans too hard upon the land,

When days seem cornered by a violent sun,
When days weigh more than two or three a time,
When rain is no more than the faintest myth

And all you do is sit inside and read
And live in words made soft and stretched by heat,
And squeeze the day for any minutes left.

I think my father makes his way in death,
Avoiding trouble, somehow getting by;
I think he's learned enough to say, well, "Love,"

And say it with a steady even voice,
And hover in it, like a bird of prey,
And look down here, where summer scolds us all,

Creatures of mud, as he well knows by now,
All cut with cracks, as he once was back then
When he would walk the earth in heavy sun.

But days go bad; thick light falls hard and long;
And questions rot before an answer comes.
This summer's worse than any I have known:

The sun grows vaster with each sallow day.
My father ages fiercely in his death.
No breath of rain to blur the cracks in mud.

GRIEF

Grief wipes away wild days that burned
Like matches struck on windy streets
    And time goes blank.

Grief scrapes dry grit across your bread
And has you swallow mother's pins
    Lost years ago.

Grief slumps upon your sagging heart:
It has all channels play white noise
    And voids the mind.

In grief the world pulls up its roots;
Life bleeds from fattened days ahead
    And hours clot.

In grief brute hills seem fragile things
And light lies dead on dusty blinds
    And voices hurt.

In grief the son walks through his town,
Through narrow angles of his mind,
    And sees no one.

Grief sidles up to you at night
And sits with you and sleeps with you
    While others fade.

In grief you thickly stay in bed
Or walk in circles, lost, although
    The road goes straight.

OLD CROW

Hey ho, old crow,
Where do you go?
I watch you fly
Wherever I go,
Old crow,
But can't keep up,
You fly too high:
Perhaps you know,
Old crow,

Where father is,
He's in your eye
Because you travel so,
He's gone from me
Old crow,
I can't keep up, I know,
Tell me
Where father is, old crow,
Show me your eye,

Show him so I can see,
See him, old crow,
In your black eye —
Show only this
So I can know,
And keep me up, old crow,
Then fly,
Fly high in thick black sky,
Old crow.

ECLIPSE

All night I hear rain puckering the lake.
Where are you, father, in these ragged hours?
Your death eclipses God: I see a flare —
Then darkness slowly walking on the water.

AGAIN

My father weeps. He looks at me, in me,
And wants it all again: the buckthorn job,
A marriage flaring every now and then,
Outlandish birds that squeal of hope and loss,
Dry winds that whip through bones, mosquito gangs
Falsettoing in hot, dark rooms at night.

I'm heading south on a wild train that snorts
And thunders through a slit in Illinois;
The darkness parts for me. He follows hard,
Outside in rain whenever I peer out.
He tells me, Look: you are your father's son.
He's right; I'm worn. I want it all again.

DOWNSTAIRS

There was a room downstairs where father went,
Where darkness smelled of coal and paraffin,
Where Christmas pudding brooded in a box.

It's where the lost things go, my father said,
When putting on his clips one graveyard shift,
I'll take you there one evening, boy, not now.

But he forgot: I'd see his shadow flare
Across the wall when stealing down at night,
When I was meant to be slum deep in dream.

How could so many lost things fit in there?
It's like the TARDIS! But all crammed with shelves
That stretch as far as Ford's, and they're all filled

With crazy stuff: Grandfather's drippy pipe
Left somewhere on the tube at Stepney Green,
Umbrellas, keys, old Tom's tobacco cards,

A sheriff badge beside a Milkybar,
My uncle's Jolly Golly in mid-swing,
Torn copies of *The Beano* dropped in parks . . .

Then I forgot; and slowly climbed my years
Like stairs that rise toward a single bulb
That's likely on the blink more times than not.

One day I'll travel back and see that house
And stand outside awhile and take it in
And maybe ask if I can go inside.

One day I'll get the key I never found.
One day I'll open up that door and look.
One day I'll find my father in that room.

2

LITTLE SONGBOOK
OF THE DARK ONE

Tonight your breath smells of the autumn rain
That ran barefoot on grass all afternoon.
We're amateurs in life, so thunderclouds
Will trouble us each time they come our way.
We don't know how to love, or even let
The rain complete its work inside our words;
Yet when I watch the rain, Dark One, I'm home,
And when we touch, I also touch the rain.

You're not prepared to hear of him: Dark One.
You cannot see him with those eyes of yours.
Your words, big locks on little glimmerings.
You hear the slow, dark turning of a storm
And not the darker words he breathes in you.
You hear me speak, and say, "Too sweet by half!"
And never know that drawing close to him
Is licking honey on a razorblade.

Late autumn, Dark One, and the mind is hard.
It sees dun leaves go past, all whipped by wind,
And thinks the dead should be content with death:
Those beery leaves and whiskey leaves must leave,
Old violin leaves, lost jockey leaves as well,
Thin trees with worried leaves and gold leaf too,
Burnt apple leaves, dirt leaves with cracking veins.
Late autumn, Dark One, and my mind's a whip.

One half of me is here; the other half
Must wait a little longer to be born:
And so I let the silence nest in me
And lower myself down into myself.
I gaze at gum trees, older than ten wars,
And cold air blossoms with a magpie's call.
I read of fighting in your book, but you,
Dark One, you doodle clouds all afternoon.

All morning long, the valley's sleepy breath,
And at my feet, young grass with fine white hair;
All morning long I look, and sip my time:
The sun snagged on a gatepost for a while,
One of those little towns turned way down low.
All afternoon, my scalene heart, Dark One,
My mind that runs and clatters after you,
And then all night the wild track of your love.

Wind works all night; deep snow is pumiced smooth
Above fine ice that wants us on our backs.
It's black and white out there, but I see love
In filigrees of snow near lumpy cars.
Ah, so you're there, Dark One, and here as well,
In flames that leap a little in my grate,
And in my lover's legs across my lap:
For hours my hands caress those curves of snow.

There is a blue through which I fall all day
When stretching out on fat, rich summer grass,
And you are there, behind it all, they say,
Like backing on a mirror one can't see.
Dark One, I look for you these afternoons;
You're here, I know, with birds that cross the sky,
Rapt sunlight riding on their wings. I taste
Those clouds that lick up all the cream on Earth.

Death's never late, Dark One, you're good that way,
Always on time, give eighty years or so.
It comes in pains I can't explain, in gaps
Between the doctor's words, and in regret:
Glass paper scratching hard against the heart.
Death's never late; it's in the waiting room,
Then brings me to a blank, cold sea to brood
And wrenches my slow head to look for you.

It's late, and so I go to be with you.
I sit awhile, alone, and slowly fall
A mile or two into myself, Dark One,
Until I reach the silence that is you.
I think of people out in Arkansas
Who walk around at dusk, in skirts of dust,
And put on lights in long abandoned homes,
And feel a little less alone out there.

The windows whisper for an hour or two
And then a silence walks around the house,
And somehow you're inside it, that I know,
Because my words go quiet when you're here.
Dark One, I sit alone without a light
And let the darkness bring me close to you:
I hear my heart switch to a smaller drum,
I listen to the paddocks slowly breathe.

Charlottesville-Tarrawarra,
2011–15

3

NORTHERN NIGHTS

On nights when snow falls fast
On nights all pupil black
    God pauses too:

At night in thickest snows
The universe must look
    For other loves,

And proofs of God that click
When read in any book
    Sprawl open wide,

All night they lay askew
When snow piles up in yard
    And just gets worse,

Each heavy bough in cast,
While wind takes off its gloves
    Out back of house

And thrashes snowflakes hard,
Those flakes that ride the black,
    While we watch too.

FEBRUARY

1

Long days of steady snow: a lake of it.
I look out from my kitchen window, cold,
And might as well be in a glass of milk.
And then I hear a bough of black oak snap.

2

I step outside and watch snow glitter down.
It's smoothed away low walls, a child's old bike
Thrown on the drive. No mailbox before long.
But nothing blunts these angles in my heart.

3

Evergreen bush: each single leaf encased
In ice, and each one sings your name, Dark One.
I try the same when looking out at night
But see my life: between two flakes of snow.

4

Wet snow is falling, stretching out the day.
I'll read the whole of Proust before night comes!
I am the guest of ink all afternoon.
Come evening, no trace of that old bough.

5

No power now: the house is icy black.
I'm wearing two thick sweaters and fur gloves
And reading at the window in snow light:
The hours are frozen hard and hardly move.

6

At two a.m. the window's bright with snow.
Outside, my neighbors sleep inside their car
And turn it over every now and then.
No sleep for me: my pillow's made of snow.

7

Only cold coffee in the fridge to drink
But Lord how good it is when half asleep!
Black bread and butter make a decent meal.
A deer comes by: its quick eye pierces me.

8

A light flicks on and then the furnace groans.
Already men are digging for their cars.
I'm somewhere layers deep beneath old clothes,
Hard as a needle, heading into town.

THE PROBLEM OF EVIL

The Problem of Evil's doing well these days:
Five international meetings in one year!
I'll skip that one in India next spring,

Calcutta's too depressing: I threw up
For two whole weeks last time, and legless kids
Kept hanging right outside our hotel door.

Smart people here in Rome; I loved those grads
Who formalized transworld depravity,
And that young Finn was maximally cute

The way she sat up by the bar, legs crossed,
Surrounded by restricted standard guys,
One with a knockdown argument, he thought,

To get her into bed. Helsinki — yes,
I think I'll stretch to that and stay awhile.
Last time they had a blowout banquet there,

The Roast Fawn Breast was tops. "It's just tofu,"
Anne reassured us all. "I'm not quite clear
What Chinese poets have to do with it,"

Quipped George, then smiled around portcullis teeth.
Weird guys, those Brits; and, Lord, their dentistry!
Non-optimal! And that odd smell they have,

But then I've seen an Oxbridge college bath
And talk of horrors that you can't defeat!
Well, here's my flight at last. Thanks Templeton,

And thanks Great Problem that We Cannot Solve!
Just think: Helsinki's not too long a wait
And I've a brand new line I want to try.

THE FUTURE

My friends, we're fucked: dark matter's everywhere,
Inside our pockets and between our teeth,
Dark energy is pushing things apart,

Yet Alpha Centauri's heading here right now
And one fine day it's gonna bang us hard
And hit our bunch of stars right out the park.

We'll get a bigger black hole then and, Lord,
Those things just let the cosmos go to hell.
There's nothing Captain Kirk can do 'bout that.

Pull out investments in the "Steady State,"
Ol' Big Bang's had the numbers now for years;
As for the "Universe," give me a break,

It's got less unity than *Blue Poles* has,
With lines of zeroes way beyond belief:
Whichever way you look, it's blank on blank.

Myself, I'd rather have the Borg than truth,
Those guys reminded me of boarding school.
No point in moving to Enceladus

When things get hot: its balmy days won't last.
So best sink dough in time machines, I'd say,
And find ourselves a pleasant piece of past,

Or slide into another world — that's cool —
One with no black-out-spots when using cells,
And do it quick, before that comet comes,

Because our very days are numbered, friends:
I hear the cosmos hissing, and the moon
Plays ring-a-ring-a-rosy with us all.

MY DEATH

Maybe my death is
Something so banal
I wouldn't see it:
A moth worrying
A flame all evening,
A dumb boy out west
Drawing short, thick lines
With blunt charcoal sticks,
Getting filthy black.

Sometimes, late at night,
I tear up my name,
Feed it to the fire,
Or scrawl over it
With shards of warm coal,
Then bathe until dawn:
Deep in the morning
I hear light wings whirr
And my name comes back.

HEAVEN: A MEMOIR

I sang it — *Holy, Holy, Holy* — heart
All out of tune, at Thomas Arnold School,
And every time my best friend Bob would fart
And slyly look around, and play the fool;

And yet I tried my best at "Casting down
Their golden crowns around the glassy sea,"
Although the nearby air smelt vaguely brown
And George picked at a scab right on my knee,

And even then I thought it rather odd
To think of all those saints, each dressed in white,
All hurling crowns about: "You stupid sod,"
St Paul might say (I thought he'd be uptight),

"Your crown just got me, here, above the eye!"
(He'd gesture to a Power on patrol
Who'd flutter over, through a cloudless sky,
And kick me downstairs, like a clod of coal.)

And older, when I sang the hymn at Mass,
Those lines would make me lean inside and muse
If names were penned by Angels during class
Then stuck on tightly with Seraphic glues

So that retrieval might be far less fraught
For those whose crowns bounced high into the sea;
But still I saw a beach where saints all fought
Each for his crown, each one a killer bee,

All crying "*Mine!*," and I, by Grace, could hear,
"It reads '*St Gregory of Nyssa*,' fool,"
"Not '*Gregory the Great!*'" Then came a jeer,
And then: dogmatic punches in a pool.

How long before they get their crowns again?
And do those labels peel away? Beats me.
These days my faith in saints is on the wane:
All day I scour for scrap beside the sea.

PRAYER

It's not too late, Dark One,
    For you to come
    And hold me close
And stay an hour or two;

It's not too late at all
    For you to slip
    Past fossil light
And quickly touch my hand.

It's deepest night, Dark One,
    I look straight up
    And won't be born
Another billion years

If you're so far away;
    Come closer now
    So that I taste
Your breath: I have been here

On tiptoe all the night,
    And I shall wait
    For you, Dark One,
Till all those years are done.

MORNING RAIN

Come little rain with morning light
And wake me just enough to see;
Come closer now, sit on my hand,

And bring whatever calm you can
So I can climb the cloudy day;
The window's open, baby rain,

Big day will blossom in wet heat,
Young wasps will cruise around at noon
And men will taste rich syrup air:

Come share the last of night with me
Before I snap into myself,
Come nuzzle coldly on my cheek.

You're coming too, dark bird, I know:
You wake me just enough to wish
That night be longer than it is,

And if it must be hard today,
Bring me a pain that sharpens mind
So I can see the world I made,

This house of books, lost in a breath
Or less than that, a little song
A small bird tries in morning rain.

4

DARKNESS

Some journeys never promise a return:
  You set out late, barefoot, at night,
    Through oblique hours
    Themselves in flight;

And there are journeys without ways at all:
  You pass through wastes of withered heath,
    Through arguments
    Like a comb's teeth;

Then there are journeys that you cannot take:
  You chew raw flesh on both your thumbs,
    You tilt your glass
    And darkness comes.

THE EMPTY CHAIR

Around an empty chair
    Sunning itself out back,
        Left for the birds,

A journey slowly feeds
    On little thoughts: I think
        Of thick, gray hairs,

Grandfather's sleeping arm
    On summer afternoons
        When he sat there;

I see thin coins brought back
    Alive from Africa,
        The ones they use

To buy a damaged soul;
    I hear the darkness sigh
        Though it is noon,

Look at the empty chair
    From deep inside a house
        That stands on stilts,

And go to sit on it
    And know that fine old heat
        All dripping thought

And almost eat my fill:
    See, I can walk this far
        And further still.

SLANT

1

A shadow slanted on the windowsill
When I was home alone one afternoon.
The kitchen breathed there in the dark awhile,

Some glasses I was drying with a cloth
Slipped back into another world I knew
When I was four, or when I fell through words,

And all at once I knew that you and I
Were shadows growing on each other's face,
Shadow on shadow making up a book

That I could read now in a single glance:
Old specters passing through our wedding snaps
And new ones coming, just as cold as truth;

So heart retreats into its cage of bone,
Starved memories return, like cornered beasts
Deep in a cave with eyes that slash the dark.

Bad days are drawing near, our table said,
And somehow slipped into a distant past
With children eating rice and laughing hard

At silly words that skipped across the day:
Some words are corridors, said glass of milk
Then leaned into the longest kiss of all,

But not for you, said window looking down,
No, not for you, sang mirror in my voice.
Some words can leave a door ajar, tried cup,

But doors can close just by themselves, droned door,
And looked at me with his fierce lock and chain.
Then shadow said, *I'm here, I'm here for good.*

No words are left, my love, no words at all,
No flowing words, no shadow of a word,
But only words already touched by night

Without the breath to say a single thing,
Exhausted words that poured their meaning out,
Summer and winter, till a story grew

And pushed itself between us at the end.
Now only hours of your face and mine,
Now only scratch words, scar words, scabby words,

Mixed with a grieving older than our years
That multiplies itself when evening comes:
No place where smells and sounds are fully known,

No children breathing softly in the night.
No words are left for that, just wounded words
That crouch inside the memory all day.

My love, when we were young I cut my hand
And let a little pear of heavy blood
Fall in a bowl that I was beating hard,

The smallest drop of blood in chocolate mix,
A charm that you might stay in love with me:
One of our children's birthday cakes it was,

And all was eaten, quick as knives can cut,
Except your slice untouched upon a plate,
Until the trash was lumped into a bag,

The children gone to bed, the silence raw
That summer evening, and nothing said
About the cake or band-aid on my thumb.

3

It was your silence snowing in the house,
Your thunder on a simmer all the day,
A storm for years forecast that never came:

And so more years of living in a "No"
With thoughts that this grim man is somehow me,
As though I'd come apart in my own hands.

It was those days that start with slamming doors,
Regret that opens, closes, all night long,
Intricate valves that let thick darkness in,

And arguments that flew around our house
And pissed on everything that you can touch
So that our place was never clean again.

It was a sorrow that corrupts each cell,
And vodka in its rampage through hot blood,
Each heart a knot that's tightened every day,

And acid looks that burned through sentences
And leached away all tenderness from lips,
And fiercer silences that ate words whole.

It was my spirit fraying in worn flesh,
A fog that seemed to come from far beneath,
A life to undergo and never live;

It was wild spring, with pollen of no hope,
Warm nights through which I fell into myself
And saw my selves withdrawing as I dropped.

And now it is a single hair, dyed red,
Still clinging to a shirt you gave me once.
See how I lay it on my windowsill.

APART

Above me in the night
My unknown neighbors walk
Across a creaking floor
    And sometimes fight:

They shout in splattered red
And speak for hours in tongues,
Without me knowing why
    They sob in bed,

And when they go away
On summer nights I hear
Their neighbors higher up
    Act their fierce play.

I don't see anyone:
And yet I still believe
In all that jagged love
    And love undone

And thinly live all week
And listen long and hard
To words from higher still
    And just as bleak.

MY DAUGHTERS

My daughters live far other lives these days;
They're weeping differently in their thin beds,
Their shadows camp all week beneath their eyes
    And star in dreams.

Their parents are a broken radio
With all its tangled wires exposed at once,
Ruined, still jabbering a talk-show gig
    No one can grasp.

My daughters dwell inside those silences
That billow up when bitter things get said,
They've heard the bass line of their parents' love
    And can't forget.

Their parents grieve and cleave and leave for good —
We were one single thing, a glass that broke
Into a maze of cracks and fell apart
    At one slight touch.

My daughters glare in thick block capitals
And shout from distant planets never seen,
Their words serrated with unhappiness
    And meant to maim.

Their parents sit and sob into their hands
As darkness slowly infiltrates each room;
We look and see for once the lines that bend
    And those that don't.

5

LITTLE SONGBOOK

It is your hand I love
Alive upon your knee
Only your naked hand

(It runs right up your neck
When we are deep in talk)

A hand with fingers stretched
And roughing up your hair
It makes you naked too

(Your fingertips will sleep
Upon my thigh tonight)

I think your hands in talk
Fashion something small
Invisible and wild

(But death can see it well
And quietly leaves the room)

I want to kiss you, love,
Under the monkey puzzle tree
Where no one ever goes
(The branches hardly move an inch,
Light bows to enter there)

But it's a puzzle, love,
To get you to that sleepy tree
When you just want to read
(I run a finger down your thigh,
My shadow blacks your page)

How cool it is there, love,
Under the monkey puzzle tree,
How good to taste its seed
(I feel the fine bones in your hand
While walking over there)

At night the only words I want to say
Are those already tempered by our love:

Bold words that venture high upon my tongue
When it is somewhere lost inside your mouth

Words that I whisper deep between your thighs
Words flying fast into wet darkness there

Fine words all shining through the palest breath
When I've lived twice or thrice within your kiss

Small words that blossom only close to hush
Or leap out through the dark in sudden cries

Old words that go to bed with us each night
Young words that taste of morning light and you

We love those liquid August days so much:
They cling like cotton shirts all limp with sweat.
September comes, and then we miss their touch.

We miss the fleshy thunderstorm's vague threat,
Thin girls who taste of Beaujolais at night:
They cling like cotton shirts all limp with sweat,

Though morning sees them gone, as well it might.
Summer restrings our days and plays them slow
With girls who taste of Beaujolais at night,

Who whisper thickly that they love you so,
Like Blues sung soft and sweet out in the dark.
Summer restrings our days and plays them slow

On yellow afternoons lost in a park . . .
I knew a girl whose very smile was wine,
Was Blues sung soft and sweet out in the dark;

She left one day without a single line.
We love those liquid August days so much:
They give us girls whose very smiles are wine.
September comes, and then we miss their touch.

So Sorrow bums his way right into town,
So Sorrow comes our way with rusty crown;
It's down oh down, my dear, it's always down.

He's got our faces fixed in his blank look,
He's got our names clean written in his book,
He's got our Queen, our Knight, he's got our Rook.

You said you loved me, and you told a lie,
But, girlfriend, on each wall there hangs a fly:
It made me hurt, dear heart, it made me cry.

But tears won't warm my bed at night, old love,
I've had it plenty, girl, I've had enough,
What's past is dead and won't bear thinking of.

And I don't care if we must call it quits,
At least I'll nail some sense into my wits,
But how you lied, sweet girl, shook me to bits.

(after a line by Son House)

A shadow stretches just behind your smile:
Your little trouble's coming home one day.
No lock will work, and hiding's not your style;
A shadow stretches just behind your smile.
At night, at noon, I'm coming mile by mile,
So don't you ever think to run away.
A shadow stretches just behind your smile:
Your Little Trouble's coming home one day.

I feel your nakedness inside your kiss
(And once I nearly died inside your kiss)

All day the sky just lazes on the sea
And I am swimming in that tide, your kiss

How everything I see is soaked with time
(But in your arms I've always sighed "Your kiss!")

It's summer and the days peel to their skin
And naked half the day I ride your kiss

At night my walnut tree soaks up the dark
(Just as one night in bed you lied your kiss)

Death has its fundamentalists as well
But I shall take another guide: your kiss!

The heart is ringing in its spire of bone
(Then pushes time aside — just for your kiss)

Now one day soon I'm going to that river
No fishing and no swimming in that river
That river flowing by without a name

I'll lose my name while crossing that old river
No day to come the other side of the river
That river running without praise or blame

I'll sing your name when riding that deep river
I'll see you linger in the light of the river
That river richly rolling all the same

My love remember me across the river
As I approach the dark side of the river
That river rushing by without a name

PARTIAL ECLIPSE

Late summer, over forty years ago,
    I went with friends to laze around
        Some reeds beside a stream,
    The evening overfull with time,

And simply lay there looking, talking low.
    Next week we'd go our ways: three boys,
        A girl with whiskey lips;
    And words came thin with that eclipse,

And there was nothing much at all to see,
    But life was waiting there, immense,
        Impatient, at each home,
    And other words began their hum.

Tonight I look out from my peeling porch
    And know those same old waves of heat,
        Taste bourbon with a lick,
    And feel again her slow, torn look.

SUMMER IN MELBOURNE

Don't go to Paris, love: it's full of punks
From Harvard, trying out their thin, bruised French.
Their cheese is chocker with cholesterol,

And that strong coffee makes your teeth go brown,
Croissants cause cancer, and smoky seminars
Reduce your life by twenty years at least.

Far better, love, to soak in summer here;
And, if you like, I'll buy a wedge of *brie*,
A bag of fresh plump cherries, a cheeky white,

And we'll read Rimbaud at St Kilda Beach
And really get inside his *cabaret*.
Don't go to Rome! Don't even talk of *that*!

My dearest, *think*: their pasta's fattening,
And Italy's one sweaty queue to see
What's up in Grandma's attic anyway!

You'll be touched up while on a crowded bus!
You'll catch a cold inside those catacombs!
There's better pizza down on Rathdowne Street

And Sapienza's really just a set
They use for B-class films like *Left Behind*:
I'll smear some olive oil across my lips

And read Montale all the afternoon!
Ah stay with me, my love, and let warm days
Just dangle overhead all summer long,

We'll sleep in late, be *louche*, and stagger through
A case or three of Yarra Valley red
And love the city and each other too.

LITTLE BOOK OF EARLY LOVE

1. Barefoot

Sweet grass, still warm,
And you

Barefoot
Beneath the lightest dress:

No words to say,
No words

Worth saying;
Only you,

White feet
Loosely laced with green,

And I,
Tasting a little sweat

Upon my lip
And looking up again:

All summer grass,
O love.

2. After Reading Herrick Together

Spring froths the field

And I am high on love
For you,
            And half asleep
In your warm arms
Near insect psalms

When day is sealed

By your light weighted words
For me,
            Who cradles them
Then lets them play
In champagne day —

May we be healed

Of bruises left by years
Alone,
            And hidden scars
That ache at night:
Love, hold me tight

For day must yield

3. Her

By wicked chance
I saw her: white
Thin panties — that is all,
And a door closed.

Later,
She sat beside me, skirt
Rucked up
About her thigh:

I touched her there,
The party
Darkly smoldering
All night.

Hard years since then
And I'm the same,
Too much
The same:

I climb my unlit stairs
And go to sleep
Alone
And it is her I see.

POOR LITTLE SOUL

(after Hadrian)

Poor little soul all lost: you were my guest,
The fine friend of my flesh.
                              Where since, so pale,
So stiff, so naked? No fun now in the dark.

THE CANON

I loved the canon more than booze and sex.
Old Eccles set the tone when I was young:
"Only one piece will steer you straight," he said,

"'Tradition and the Individual Goon'";
But I had English cornered, day and night,
And I recall the time it first came on —

At Last the F. R. Leavis Show! "Oh fuck,
Do turn it off: I'm reading Shelley's *Ode!*"
My girlfriend yelled, and sent me down the pub

To buy a bag of crisps; there, free inside,
I found a tiny Alexander Pope
("Hey kids, collect them all!"). We bought huge packs

But never found the one we wanted most:
John Keats, complete with bloody handkerchief.
"Have you read *DHL* (nudge nudge, wink wink)?"

A tweedy man with pipe asked at the bar.
Well, there was time enough to chat with him
And place a bet on who could précis Proust

In under thirty seconds. Mostly, though,
I read the sagas — bloody Vikings! — then
Slipped into town to get some eggs and spam.

Don't get me wrong: I love the moderns too,
Old Tom with his litotes, parody —
Oh he knew all the tricks, and had the Grail

Up in his digs, beside a comfy chair.
I love it all, from Harry to John Cleese!
I love the canon! Got that? Now piss off!

ALMOST CLASSICAL

1

Wake little one and hold me tight.
So, did you dream of me last night?
Or maybe you prefer to sulk
      Because we fight?

I know you keep a little book
That shows how much I really took
From pretty girls, and how I was
      Lit by each look:

Girls with lynx eyes, espresso hair,
Blonde girls well worth a double dare,
Whose kisses tasted of old Scotch
      Or juicy pear.

You'll tell me that I've been a dill
And never knocked a single thrill;
Well, you're a pilgrim soul, I know,
      And a grim pill

Especially when I sleep in
And dump the whole damn day in bin,
But I'll bet big on fucking girls
      And I will win.

2

Congratulations, Flesh, you're doing well
    For someone on the way to hell;
        But life, you know, is short
        And not all sport:

You may not like me hanging round at night
    When you have satin blondes in sight,
        But I am stuck with you,
        Shall see things through.

Forgive me if I must avert my eyes
    And close my ears to all your lies,
        And, worse, your self-deceit
        When you're in heat:

You've got a little while, it's true, to live
    And take far more than you will give,
        But God will not be bucked
        And we'll be fucked.

MERCI

O thank you, Michel Henry: when I spoke
Of you, *la vie*, and all, I caught her eye,
And, well, it wasn't long at all before

We met one day to read *Un coup de dés*,
So *merci aussi, maître*: your bright lines
Helped keep her pretty hand beside my own.

And thank you, Maurice Blanchot! We talked of you
For half an afternoon before we kissed,
And I will never blank those seconds, nor

The minutes after them in time to come.
And Marcel Proust, I thank you most: your words
About those orchids gave me an idea

I shouldn't mention in a poem, not
On this side of the grave (or, worse, that side),
But one that made my sweetheart smile then laugh

Then go much further than I had in mind.
Mon coeur, let's leave the University
To wicked Deans and Devils for a spell,

Let's go to Saint-Barthélemy, and let
Our French get tanned a little in the sun,
Admire Gustavia while sipping Kir

And let the trade winds lick our burning arms.
Verlaine's *Cythère* will be our only text
But folded up and left on board the plane,

Because, *chérie*, I read more Proust last week
And want to whisper some of his sweet words
Inside your ear the moment we're in bed.

HAPPINESS

Perhaps my happiness is
This thin October light,
A gray-cheeked thrush
And love's dark places where
Bright words make nests.
How quickly pixels skim
Your image from your face,
The coolness of your neck,
Your cotton dress
Loose on your back.

How slowly old Earth turns;
I'm sitting on a ridge
In soft Virginia,
You're perching on that broken shell,
Antarctica. My love,
The fat Earth moved
A little faster when we laughed —
My life was cream;
But when I looked
October was October still.

That gray-cheeked thrush
Flew right up on a branch
And sang to me:
Perhaps your happiness is
Our great Earth turning
To bring you back
So you can taste her lips
While slipping off
Her cotton dress
In warm December light.

SUGAR

Today I want a life
That's sweet, without a thought,
Like sunlight idling in
The dripping grass, or like
A sugar cube that slides
Into my first Typhoo.

Fine summer raindrops brush
My bedroom window, feel
Like lips and fingertips
And slip through my half-sleep,
That starry cave that's lit
With images of you.

Some words have locks on them
But not the words I want,
All made of air: bright words
To talk with to the rain
And sing a little, too,
Of sunlight, sugar, you.

As warm air sips huge clouds
That fade all afternoon
In Africas of light,
So there are lazy days
In which I melt in you:
Fine days and long days, full
Of kisses plush with wine.

You're drinking tea today,
Green tea with a long spoon,
The sun a pomegranate
Split open, dripping red,
And half an hour floats by:
A cube of sugar falls
And shatters on the floor.

My girl's asleep
And tall rain guards her room

(My shadow drags
Its zeroes everywhere)

You'll quite dissolve!
O Sugar, don't come out!

(My shadow weeps
Licks wet grass tenderly)

I hereby vow
To keep my sugar dry!

(A filthy day
Just fell all over me)

Huge sun gets high
Her shadow hugs her feet

(Hey, Sugar, see
You made the big day shine!)

A storm lets down its hair
But no one's climbing up:
We're staying in today
And making love, I hope,

But first I make some tea
(There is a swollen pause)
And put the sugar out,
And then we stop, because

It starts to hail outside
(And sounds like sugar's fall
Into an empty cup).
You wrap up in your shawl,

And drink your tea too fast
And look up at the clock:
"I'm cold," you say, all eyes,
And quickly turn a lock.

The sugar glitters in its bowl;
A tulip sings its cut-glass song.
(A moment stops, but nothing's wrong.)

You came inside an hour ago:
Your face was flattered by the cold.
(I stirred the sugar, fold on fold.)

The tulip sways to spring's deep soul;
Some baby leaves just test the skies.
(The sugar parties in your eyes.)

Ask me about the sugar cane
That burns on summer evenings
Just south of Innisfail,
How its immense perfume
Enters the deepest mansion of the soul:
You don't need wine, my friend,
You don't need rum.

And ask about the sugar ants
Swarming beneath the sheets up there —
Burnt orange on your legs,
Black heads that stare you down
While quickly sucking on your sweaty hairs:
You'll need a drink, my friend,
You'll need some rum.

But never ask about her kiss
That tastes like naked sugar juice,
Or how, one harvest night,
She slipped her panties, warm,
Beneath my head so I might have sweet dreams:
I don't need wine, my friend,
I don't need rum.

Let's fuck in French today,
Mon sucre: kiss
Me thinking lacy things
In *Marseillais, Suisse,*

Or any tongue you like!
O lick me there
Bien jeune fille, bonbon,
But please don't stare —

I'm English to my roots!
Perhaps, *fille douce,*
We'll simply start again
With something *louche* —

Is that good French, *chérie?*
— *Mon malabar!*
— *Ah, suce ma canne à sucre*
Plus bas, plus bas . . .

Angel of summer, Tariel,
How sad you look today:
Your wings hang limp with rain.

O Ampiel, bright Sugar Bird,
I leave my tea-set bowl
Uncovered all night long!

Now that the days are shrinking fast
I see only a sparkle
Dancing on my spoon.

Angels are leaving us in droves!
It's cold and gray at noon
And feathers rise in tea.

But you, sweet girl, are coming home
This frozen afternoon:
I feel you drawing close,

O angel of the deepest kiss,
In broken steps through snow,
In winter's fallen light.

There's sugar in your eyes
And sugar in my blood
And sugar too, somehow,

When sugar gliders swim
Through yards of velvet air

A luster in your eyes,
A riot in my blood
And yet I see, somehow,

The sugar glider's claws
That bite a tree for sap

I slowly kiss your eyes,
Your scarlet nails in bud
And start to know, somehow,

The insects at their hymn
The gliders' hidden lair

I'm thinking with my eyes,
My thoughts cut through a cloud,
And then at once, somehow,

We break a few old laws
I glide you to my lap.

You stupid rain, fat rain,
No one likes you!
The baby sparrows cry
Cars splash away

You trashy lowlife rain
Stomping on grass
And in small nests too full
No one likes you!

Old broken tattered rain
Hard-working rain
In the mucky garden
Well, maybe stay

Sweet rain, o kindly rain,
Doodle all day
Chill until evening comes
Keep Sugar here